I0813312

Advent and Christmas with Mother Angelica

Also by Mother Angelica

Praying with Mother Angelica: Meditations on the Rosary, the Way of the Cross, and Other Prayers

Mother Angelica's Answers, Not Promises

Mother Angelica on Christ and Our Lady

Mother Angelica on Suffering and Burnout

Mother Angelica on God, His Home, and His Angels

Mother Angelica's The Way of the Cross

Mother Angelica's Quick Guide to the Sacraments

Mother Angelica's Guide to Practical Holiness

A Holy Hour with Mother Angelica

Mother Angelica on Prayer and Living for the Kingdom

Mother Angelica's Guide to the Spiritual Life

Mother Angelica's Lessons on Genesis

What Is Heaven?

In His Sandals: A Journey with Jesus

Living the Scriptures

Mother Angelica's Keys to the Interior Life

Mother Angelica Talks It Over

Mother M. Angelica

Advent and Christmas with Mother Angelica

EWTN Publishing, Inc.
Irondale, Alabama

The chapters in this book are taken from *Mother Angelica Live*.

Cover design by LUCAS Art & Design, Jenison, MI.

On the cover: *Adoration of the Child by Mary, St Joseph and Shepherds* by Tommaso Lunetti (1490–1564), public domain / Wikimedia Commons.

EWTN Publishing, Inc.
5817 Old Leeds Road, Irondale, AL 35210

Distributed by Sophia Institute Press
Box 5284, Manchester, NH 03108.

paperback ISBN 978-1-68278-433-4
ebook ISBN 978-1-68278-434-1

Library of Congress Control Number: 2025944566

First printing

Contents

Advent

Christmas

Advent

The Spirit of Christmas

When I was a kid, I used to hate Christmas—and Thanksgiving. You know why? Well, when you're poor, and you're not too sure where you're going next, or what's going to happen, when you live without the bare necessities of life, holidays are very difficult. Did you know that? They're very difficult.

If you've lost your husband and you two used to have such a good time on Christmas, then you don't look forward to Christmas anymore. If you know your mother and father can't get you what you like—you want that big bike, and you want this, and you want that, and you see all these other kids running around with all kinds of gifts—you don't look forward to Christmas. And all of these things pile up in our lives.

And I wondered, "Why?" As I look back, I can see I had the wrong idea of Christmas.

You know, we all have the wrong idea of Christmas. We just automatically think that Christmas is a fun time. And sometimes it is. But you get kind of angry because some people have wonderful Christmases. And then you look at those people and you look at yourself, and it can be a tremendously depressing day.

So we have to find out: What is your spirit of Christmas? You see, in my day, if I had the right spirit of Christmas, those things—and that's all they were: things, even food—wouldn't have mattered too much to me. It wouldn't have meant so much that it was a depressing day. If I would have thought of Whose birthday it was, if I would have known that that Little Baby was the Son of God and that He was mine, that He came for me, if I had known that the Eternal Father sent His Son just for me, it would have taken that day, which was more a national holiday to me, and turned it around, and it wouldn't have mattered, really, whether I had something, whether I had the gift, whether we had a tree, or anything else. It would have been special in my heart, you see.

What is your spirit of Christmas? What does Christmas mean to you? Is it His birthday? Is it the birthday of Someone you love very much but, most of all, Someone that you know—maybe for the first time in your life—loves you? I mean, that's a wonderful, wonderful thing.

How are you going to go into Christmas? Are you suicidal? Do you dread Christmas? Are you looking forward to it? Well, what are you looking forward to? "I want a bike." All right. That's a material thing. But what happens if your mother or father can't buy you a bike? See, the spirit of Christmas is an inner joy. It has nothing to do with all these things around you, nothing at all.

But, you know, we got everything turned around, don't you think? If I had a birthday, you would give a gift to me, right? But you don't do that on Christmas. It's *His* birthday. And you give gifts to each other. That's kind of odd. I think we ought to go back to St. Nicholas on the sixth of December. But it's okay if that expresses your spirit, a giving spirit.

Number one, "Christmas spirit" means I understand that the Eternal Father sent Jesus down on this earth. It's a wonderful, wonderful thing that happened. And see, if I had understood He was not accepted by the people—see, that's how I felt when I was a kid: not accepted. Because my parents were divorced, I was not acceptable. Nobody understood, nobody liked it, and I was kind of pushed aside a little bit. So, I couldn't understand. Had I known, though, the real meaning of Christmas, I would have understood. And nothing else would have mattered, except that He came. He was sent by the Father.

The Expectation of Mary

In the old Church, the good ol' days, they had a feast called the Expectation of Mary, and it was on the eighteenth of December. Can you imagine the expectation of Our Lady? Unbelievable expectation, and this was the Son of God, and she knew it. It was no surprise to her.

You can imagine Our Dear Lady getting prepared and Joseph making a crib and all the things that you're doing now to prepare for Christmas. And the awesome thing about that is it never came to be. They had to leave Nazareth and go to Bethlehem. I don't think that was a surprise to Our Lady, though. She was very versed in Scripture. But all the things she prepared had to be left home. And all she could take was herself, Joseph, and a donkey. See, they intended to go and come right back.

Can you imagine the spirit of Our Lady and her absolute obedience to—*what*? To that birth. It didn't even matter to her that she couldn't have all the things she had prepared.

Let's say, for example, we've got everything prepared for Christmas, and somebody we love dies, and we have to leave and go to another state. It's like something you prepared has just kind of been squashed. Everything is over. There's no more exuberance and no more expectation, and you were going to have turkey, and you were going to do this and that, and it seems it all died. What would be your expectation then? What would be your spirit of Christmas at that point? How would you react if everything you prepared for Christmas was suddenly washed away? And you go to a city totally foreign to you, and when you get there, it's crowded, people everywhere—people, donkeys, everything, everywhere, just edging your way. You go from end to end, end to end, and there's no room, no room, no room.

You see what happened to Our Lady. The expectation that she had on the eighteenth, and which we used to celebrate, was the expectation of the birth—not all the fringe benefits around it—and knowing that her time was near. And she didn't know where to go, yet—knowing all of that—she never lost the wonder of her expectation because her mind was totally wrapped around Jesus. The birth of Jesus was the most important thing. The fact that she was disappointed, they couldn't bring a cradle, they couldn't bring all the clothes, they couldn't do anything. She had a minimum. The fact that nobody wanted them: You know, you can't even think of that. We hear this at Mass, and we just kind of slide over it. But just think now, all of you women out there, think what that would mean to you, and that expectation of Our Lady, so bound up in the will of the Father, because she said, "Be it done to me according to Thy will."

See, her spirit was alive in the will of God. So all the things around that just fell away and were a disappointment did not spoil her expectation, not for a moment. When the Infant was born, He came into the arms of a Mother unlike any other mother—pure, holy, filled with love, untouched by the disappointment, untouched by the poverty, untouched by the rudeness of all the people around her. And you see, that's what used to make my Christmas so miserable in the past when I was a kid: no tree, no gifts, nothing. But see, that was so false. I missed the whole message.

How many of you have missed the whole message? And that's what you need to ask yourself: "What is my spirit for Christmas? If everything I prepared suddenly disappeared, what would I have? Would I have that expectation of Our Lady? Would I have that love that couldn't wait for Him to be born?" And you have to remember: To God, all things are present. There's no past or future. So, on Christmas Eve when that Child is born, He is born; *again*, not again and again. But the Father sees that birth. I can see it too. I can be there. In my heart, in my mind, in my love, I can be there.

You see, that kind of Christmas nothing can take away—whether you get the same ol' tie you've got for twenty years, and your husband buys you something that doesn't fit, or somebody opens a present you bought that you thought was so wonderful, and they say, "What are we going to do with that? I wanted a bike. I got roller skates. What am I going to do with roller skates?" And these things happen. By that time, I'd take the roller skates and wrap them around his neck, you see. Say, "Hey, wait a minute! What are you talking about?"

But see, that's because all these things matter to us. We watch people open up the present that we bought, and we wait for that look. Is that what you do, huh—you look for that look? You know, you say, "I wonder if she likes this? I wonder if he likes that?" See, and you're just, oh, you're brokenhearted. And it happens to every family; it happens every time. And you shopped and shopped, and you got this for Aunt Mary, and Aunt Mary looks at it and says, "Ugh." And what happens? Your spirit of Christmas is absolutely, totally gone.

You go to Midnight Mass—if you go—and you're all disgruntled. Why? Because your Uncle Harry didn't like his orange tie. Well, who cares? He's not going to wear it anyway. You've never seen him wear a tie you bought for him. Why did you buy another one? I would never buy a tie for a man. One time I tried, and I went nuts. First of all, the clerk didn't know what I was doing, a nun buying a tie, till after I explained all of that, you know. "I don't use them. I don't want them. I'm buying it for a friend." But she kept looking at me like, "*Oh ho*, there's something wrong here." I looked at twenty thousand ties, all over the place. And she showed me one after another, and I was more confused than I was before. So, what did I do? I said, "Thank you. I think I'll get something else." By that time, she wanted to take every tie she showed me and wrap it around my neck. And we go through these kinds of things every Christmas. We never learn.

I had all these little pinwheels I gave away. After Christmas, I got them all back, plus three more. And it happens, you know. And all those things, unfortunately, have the power to spoil, to destroy, sometimes, the whole spirit of Christmas. So, I want you to think of that.

We have a custom in our country, and many countries have customs; many countries have gift giving and on different days—some on the sixth of December. Some on the sixth of January, when we have the three Magi. Since we're here in America, and this is the custom in America, I think you can do both. But the motivation for the gifts must be so different. The motivation for buying that blessed tie, and your kids a bike, and whatever you're going to buy, has to be a gift for Jesus. "What you do to the least you do to me" (Matt. 25:40).

I think in your heart there has to be that expectation of Our Lady: "He's coming. He's coming." And when you get your dinner prepared, and you've invited all the children, you have your mother-in-law and all, that shouldn't occupy the heart. Yeah, maybe occupy the mind, but not the heart.

There always has to be, even when you wake up in the morning, "He's coming." There are so many days now before He comes. If that's there and you keep it there, there's no reason for gifts or anything else to spoil that. And sometimes you can't find the right gift. But see, that shouldn't spoil it either. Be simple. Say, "Look sweetheart, Uncle John, I couldn't find you the right gift. Here's twenty-five dollars. Buy your own." We don't have to be enslaved by what's necessary, what's in our culture. We don't have to be so preoccupied that we forget Whose birthday it is. If you're going to buy your child a little toy, just say, "Baby, Jesus, I'm buying You this toy for my child." He was a baby.

And I often wonder, did He have a toy? Did He have something to play with? You say, "Well, He was God." I know He's God. But He was also a baby, an adolescent, a teenager. He was all those things, and He's yours, He's all yours, and He's all mine, and what I give for you, what I buy for you, I must do it for Him.

I think if you put that part of your enthusiasm into your gift, I think the spirit of Christmas will be stronger inside you. We make all kinds of choices. But we need to make the choice pleasing to Jesus. When you go to buy that tie, say, "Lord, which tie do You want so that I can express my love for You and my joy in Your coming through my husband [my brother, my brother-in-law, my uncle]?" Whatever it is, put Jesus into your buying. Put Jesus into that tree you're decorating.

Why don't you put a light in your window? It's a beautiful custom to say, "In this house, in the darkness of this world, there's a light in my house. My lamp is lit. I'm ready for Your coming." I think if you do those kinds of things, and you spiritualize even buying your turkey, that spirit will never leave you.

Thy Will Be Done

I want to draw a little comparison here between Zechariah and Mary. Mary knew the Mighty God. She was versed in Scripture, and she was awe-struck to know that she was chosen to be His Mother, but she was full of peace because, you know, the One she was about to bear was the Prince of Peace. Poor Zechariah was not full of peace.

You know, you can't find peace anywhere today, can you? You look at the newspaper—riots and murders and everything imaginable. You look at the world news—wars and rumors of wars and civil wars. You look everywhere, anywhere, there's no peace because peace doesn't come by law. Peace comes from the heart, and the only one who can bring peace in the heart is Jesus.

Do you know anyone who has a peaceful heart? I bet you're going to have to look a little while, kind of scratch your head and say, "Well, I think So-and-so has a peaceful heart." Well, maybe they do and maybe they don't. We don't unless we have Jesus in our hearts, unless we can do what Mary did. Most of us, though, are pretty much like Zechariah.

Zechariah was an old man, and he didn't have any children, and he'd been asking for a child for years. Every time he went to the temple, he asked for a child, but nothing. This time, it's his time to go and offer sacrifice, and there appears to him an angel of the Lord standing on the right side of the altar of incense, and the sight disturbs Zechariah, and he is overcome with fear.

Now, everybody says, "Oh, I wish I could see my guardian angel." Oh, I don't know if I wish that or not. I mean, this guy was scared to death. And the angel said to him, "Zechariah, don't be afraid. Your prayer has been heard." Now, don't you have a few prayers, and you wish an angel would come down and say, "Your prayer has been heard"? What would you do? You'd jump up and down? You'd be happy? Okay, that's what he does. And he goes on—I mean the angel's not finished with the old man—and he says, "Your wife, Elizabeth, is to bear you a son, and you must name him John" (Luke 1:13).

What would you do if you were waiting for a son for fifty years, and this angel came along and said, "Your wife is going to bear you a son"? Would you be jumping up and down? Well, he said, "Your wife, Elizabeth, is to bear you a son, and you must name him John." Oh, I mean, this man's been waiting a long time, but I don't think he thought he'd ever get this. The angel said, "He will be your joy and delight and many will rejoice at his birth. And he will be great in the sight of the Lord, and he must drink no wine or strong drink. And even from his mother's womb, he will be filled with the Holy Spirit" (Luke 1:14–15). You know how we know that for sure? Because when Mary went to visit Elizabeth, Elizabeth looked at her and said, "How is it that the Mother of my Lord should come to me?" (Luke 1:43). And immediately, *immediately*, John leaped in Elizabeth's womb. Oh, he was sanctified! "And he will bring back many of the sons of Israel to the Lord." And he says, "He will come in the spirit and the power of Elijah." Wouldn't that make you happy, huh? Would it still scare you? It probably would. "And he will go before Him to turn the hearts of fathers toward their children and the disobedient back to God" (Luke 1:16, 17).

And you know what Zechariah said? Did he say, "Oh, whoopie! Wonderful! Thank you very much. I've been waiting many years. Would you express my gratitude to the Lord God?" You know what he did? He said, "How can I be sure of this? I'm an old man" (Luke 1:18). Like, "Why didn't you come ten years ago? My wife is getting on in years." Now here is a priest of the Lord explaining the facts of life to an angel.

But we do the same thing, in other words. We say a prayer, and we really want something from the Lord, but we think in our heart, "He can't do it. He's not going to do it. It's not possible. Nothing's possible in this situation." Haven't we all done that once in a while? And then we said a kind of half-hearted prayer? And even if the Lord Himself sent somebody to say, "Now look, this is possible. It's going to be okay. Don't worry about it. Don't fret over it," we don't understand.

But just don't mess around with an angel; this angel didn't have the patience of God. He says to him, "I am Gabriel, who stands in God's presence, and I've been sent to speak to you and bring you good news. But since you don't believe in my words, which will come true in their appointed time, you will be silenced and have no power of speech" (Luke 1:19–20)—and he just zipped his lip. How do you like that? Just zipped his lip. Now, the poor man goes outside, and he can't say a word. He's been in there a long time. Did you ever stand in line for Confession and you think somebody died in there? You got that urge to knock on the door or something and say, "Are you there?" By the time they come out, you got about three or four more sins that you want to confess—like murder, impatience, see?

Well, that point has nothing absolutely to do with what I am talking about. But this man was at that point, you see, and the angel was not going to fuss around with him. Did you ever wonder what Elizabeth wondered when he came home? Did she whisper secretly, "Thank You, Lord. Thank You for small favors"? You know, the angels want us to talk to them like we would each other, but not with disbelief—never with disbelief. So if an angel appears to you, I'd be very humble, very believing, and very grateful. Otherwise, he may zip your lip.

When we get to Our Lady, the same angel goes to her. And we've talked about this before, but Scripture is something that you can read over and over. Otherwise, you'd read it once and put it on a shelf like any other book. But you can't do that. Our Lady had that grace. We just celebrated the feast of the Immaculate Conception, and I was thinking this morning during the Divine Office that the Immaculate Conception is such an awesome thing.

Some of our feminist friends have gone after the wrong thing. We should be so excited that the only sinless one besides God Himself was a woman. Now, that's something to get excited over, not the fact that if you want to climb a telephone pole, you can climb it. That's the essence of feminism. I am a feminine woman. I am a woman who was brought here by God, and so were you, for the purpose of being like that wonderful, wonderful woman we call Mary, conceived without sin, a virgin before and after the birth of Jesus. We can't even imagine such a woman.

So, when this same angel appears to her, he says the same thing. He says, "Don't be afraid." She was too humble in her heart to think that an angel would come to her with these words. He said, "Listen, you are full of grace." If you've often wondered why Catholics believe she was immaculately conceived, it was because she was full of grace. He said, "You are to conceive and bear a Son, and you must name Him Jesus, Savior." Wow! "And He will be great and will be called Son of the Most High. And the Lord God will give Him the throne of His ancestor David, and He will rule the house of Jacob forever. And there will never be an end to His reign." And when Mary said, "How can this become about?" He said, "The Holy Spirit will come upon you, and the power of the Most High will overshadow you, and the Child shall be called holy, Son of God" (Luke 1:30–35).

Well, the greatest word that's ever been said in the whole wide world, after the words of Jesus, was this word: "Be it done to me according to Thy will" (see Luke 1:38).

Making Room for Jesus and Seeing Him in Others

What are you going to give Jesus for Christmas? We give gifts to everybody on Christmas, everyone we love or know. And we do that in imitation of the Father, Who gave us Jesus. I said to one little boy, "Let's pretend it's your birthday. And I give a gift to this little girl. Would that be right?"

And he said, "Oh, no."

I said, "Well, that's what we do with Jesus."

I got a gift from someone—the Lord, to be exact—something I wanted for a long time. It's [a picture] called *El Santo Niño de Atocha* (the Holy Infant of Atocha). [In the picture], He's got a little feather in

His hat. There's a little basket. It's supposed to have bread in it. There's a water jug.

In Spain, a couple of centuries ago, there was a statue of the Bambino in the arms of Our Lady; it was called *Our Lady of Atocha*. Well, one morning, they found that the Bambino's sandals were dirty, and they thought, "Now, how did that happen?" So, they took the sandals off. He was all dressed up in clothes; that's what they do in some of the European countries. And they took His little sandals off, and they washed them and put them back on. Well, the next morning, His feet were dirty, and the hem of His garment was all muddy. That happened night after night. Well, the sexton decided he was going to find out who was doing this to the Bambino. So he put all the lights out, and he just sat there and waited, ready to grab the one who was doing all this damage. And suddenly, he saw the Bambino leave Our Lady's arms. And He had a basket full of bread in His hand, and He had a jug of water.

This is a mystery? No. I'm talking about a reality. Now, what happened was that in those days, men who were in prison were not fed by the city. Their families, and mostly children, had to go and feed them. So, what happened? Well, those who didn't have family, those who didn't have children, were not fed. So, El Niño would go every night and feed the prisoners who didn't have anything.

Now, you say, "Aw!" I can just hear my liberal friends out there. I don't know why you listen anyway. They say, "There she goes with that pietistic stuff."

Well, let me tell you about that. It's because our children have lost the reality of the tiny Jesus that they don't relate. See, when a child sees this God Who reduced Himself to this, for him, he understands. For those of you who are not Catholic and say, "Ahch! There they go worshipping plaster!"—no, it's not plaster, no more than we worship the statue of Lincoln. That's a pretty big one. Washington, Robert E. Lee: Do we worship them? No. What are they? This little Fellow is a reminder, and the Little Baby in the crib is a reminder, to you and me of the power and the love of Jesus.

Before we go on to ask what you are going to give Jesus for Christmas, let's go back a few centuries, twenty of them, and look at the world. It was cruel. People had really no value, only inasmuch as what they could produce. There was terrible, terrible immorality, dishonesty, and cruelty everywhere.

Jesus was prophesied. The coming of the Messiah was prophesied by prophet after prophet, Isaiah especially, saying that the Father would send a Redeemer. Are there any of you who would question that we need a Redeemer today? Conditions were worse than they are now, although you have a hard time figuring out how they could be worse than they are now. But there wasn't that love for God because God was so far away. He was One Who had to be pacified. So awesome was He—and He is—that they would hardly say His name. Wow! The curtain that separated the middle of the temple was so thick. It was the width of a man's hand. People then didn't have a personal relationship with God. If you're good, they thought, God will bless you. If you're not good, He will not bless you. And proof of

God's favor was many children, and wealth, peace, whatever.

Well, Jesus the Messiah was prophesied for centuries. And they were looking for Him. Now, when the Wise Men went to Herod and said, "Where is He?" and he said, "Who?" "The newborn King." Oh, what happened to him? He was scared to death.

He brings in the scribes, and he says, "Tell me, is there a new king that is to be born?"

They said, "Yes, the Messiah."

"Where?"

They said, "Bethlehem."

Do you realize that these men knew exactly where He would be born? It was prophesied that men would come from the East to worship. When the Wise Men left, those scribes did nothing. They didn't believe the prophecies they studied and studied and studied for centuries.

Isn't it strange that you and I, who know the Scriptures—I hope you do, and know the prophecies in the Scriptures—we still may miss the Second Coming? Everybody missed the First Coming, except some shepherds who were told by the angels, and the Wise Men, who followed a star. Why was it that there He was, and they never knew it? Is it possible that you and I could be seeing Him every day? Yeah, we do: in our neighbor. Is it possible that we who have the Eucharist, that wonderful Body, Blood, Soul, and Divinity of Jesus, pass Him by and say, "There is no room for You in my inn? I don't believe You're there"? Is it possible? Oh, yes. And that is the problem today. There is no room for Him today, any more than there was in His day. There are shepherds around, a lot of them, the faithful. There are some wise men. But what do you believe?

And if you believe that Infant was the Son of God, and He was, and is, what are you going to do for Him for Christmas? It is His birthday, you know. I never saw anybody who had a birthday and was ignored by so many people. You break your neck buying gifts. And the next day, almost everybody you bought a gift for returns it. It doesn't fit, for whatever reason. I wouldn't go in a store the day after Christmas if you gave me a million dollars. Well, maybe a million dollars. But, you see, we do work hard to please people. But do you remember *Whose* birthday it is?

What are you going to give to Jesus and to His Mother? How many of you wives have ever given a present—oh, this is going to knock you cold—to your mother-in-law on your husband's birthday? Oh boy! I mean, this is one big fat zero, huh? Did you ever think about it? Did you ever want to think about it? No, no, no. How many of you have given a gift to your mother on your birthday? Wouldn't that be something? Well, don't you think you should? Have you ever thought about it? Huh? Have you even said, "Mom, thanks a lot! I'm grateful"? So, while we're thanking Our Dear Lord for coming so small, let's thank His Mother, who said, "Yes, Lord" and did not fail in faith even when her Divine Son had to be born in a stable. Most of you were born either in a nice warm house or in some hospital. Well, the Son of God was born in a stable.

What are you going to give Jesus for Christmas?

If we pray together, Our Dear Lord promised, He'll be in our midst, where two or three gathered. And if you want to know what He wants you to do, just ask. He'll tell you. See, there is a value of giving. I think you're doing well in praying for others. That's intercessory prayer. We need to pray for the faithful in the Church. We need to pray for our priests and bishops and cardinals and the Holy Father. We need to pray for all those who believe in Jesus, for all Christians. We need to pray for atheists, agnostics, and those who have lost their faith, for those who try to destroy Jesus and destroy the Church and destroy our Faith and destroy your faith, those who want to rob us of everything we hold dear. We need to pray for them. That can be a beautiful gift for Jesus on His birthday.

Sometimes we don't think the best gift we can give somebody is just to go and see them and talk to them. I went to a nursing home one time years ago, and I saw this elderly woman sitting in a chair near a window, all by herself, and I went up to her, and I said, "Hi."

She said, "Hello."

I said, "Where are you from?" And she told me, and I said, "You look so sad."

"Yes," she said, "I have nine children, and not one comes to see me."

I said, "Oh, how sad!" I said, "Christmas is around the corner. Maybe they will."

And she said, "No. They won't. I've had many Christmases here. None of them have come."

You see, she didn't want a gift. She didn't want presents. She didn't want flowers. She didn't want candy. She just wanted her children. And sometimes I think we don't realize that we ourselves can be a gift to someone. Maybe you need to go to a nursing home and be a son or a daughter to someone whose children no longer care. They don't want any other gift or present. All they want is you. Try it. You'll be bringing Jesus to them in a new way.

Keeping Jesus in Christmas

A very good gift to Jesus is to want to live the Gospel. See, you got to keep Jesus in Christmas, when you eat those hams and turkeys and piggies and all the other stuff you eat. I went somewhere for Christmas, and they had a little pig they called a "pig out," and I said, "A pig out?" The best thing I ever tasted. But you need to know that you're celebrating His birthday. Most people argue, you know, newlyweds—I feel so sorry—they don't know whose house to go to, you know:

"You're coming to my mother's house."

"No. You're coming to *my* mother's house."

"Well, we'll go to your mother in the morning and my mother in the afternoon."

What a way to celebrate Christmas! You know, we argue, we fuss, we fume, we don't like the turkey. The gravy's too salty. My mother never did know how to make a pumpkin pie. It looked like a truck ran over it. Well, spoon it. Who cares if a truck ran over it? You know, she did her best. We fuss over the craziest things.

You know, the late shoppers get me. They get me, by golly. If I had a store, I'd wait for them all, then close it. I think if you haven't had the guts, the money, or the strength to do something beforehand, why are you going at eleven o'clock Christmas Eve? "Well, I'm busy." Yeah, the whole world is busy. Why do you gotta go at eleven o'clock Christmas Eve and bother everybody else? See, think ahead.

But Whose birthday is it? You know, our politicians today—oh, God help us all!—they have trees that look like they belong in concentration camps. They have everything on them but the Lord. And the reason the trees are there is not to celebrate Christmas, not to celebrate the Christ Child's birthday. It's just some kind of pagan holiday. One thing you could do is put Jesus in Christmas. It's His day. It's not your day.

My mother used to do this on Christmas: She lived right across the street from St. Peter's. And she would go and spend three hours with the Lord. There was nobody around, nobody. Beautiful tree, beautiful crib, beautiful flowers, and not a soul.

Do you ever notice everybody says around the middle of Christmas dinner, "Oh, I'll never eat again"? Then they go for the pie. "Oh, I'll never eat again." And then, they go for another piece of pie. "Oh, I'll never eat again." And there they are, two, three o'clock, and they're still eating, and they'll never eat again. So, what do they do? They take a nap. And what happens? At six o'clock, they start again.

Wouldn't it be wonderful if you sang "Happy Birthday" to Jesus at dinner or lunch or whatever you call it, and then, instead of going to sleep and then eating more, went to visit Him? Wouldn't that be wonderful? Put a little gift in the crib. Now, that would be Christmas, see?

You know, He didn't come to receive. He came to give. And He gave Himself totally because He had nothing that the world holds dear: no fine clothes, no warm house. He came to give His total self in utter poverty and humility. One day, when you and I get to Heaven, we will realize what He really did for us. We will understand.

I can't tell you how many years ago, but we used to have a little empty crib. We put it out on November 11. And every time you performed some act of virtue, you put a straw in it so that when Jesus comes, He'll have a nice soft bed. And I never saw anybody put them in, but it kept getting more straws every day. You know, I guess you kind of look around and be sure no one is going to see you put that straw in. We talked about putting straws in your little crib so that when Jesus comes, He'll have a nice soft bed. One of my sisters said to me, "Well, if you goof off, do you have to take a straw out?" No, you don't have to take a straw out. But this is a wonderful thing to do with children, because then they learn, you see? They learn devotion; they learn that they've got to give to Jesus as Jesus has given to them. So, if you haven't done anything like that this Christmas, I suggest you do something to teach your children what Christmas means.

There are all kinds of things that you can do, like say the Rosary before you open your gifts. And some of you know what's in that box. You've got the same box every year. Men get lots of ties and sweaters, and I don't know what women get, but there's just so many things you can buy somebody, you know? But the thing is that we're going to do something for Him, Whose birthday we celebrate, before we start ripping open those packages. And that's what we all want to do.

As I said when I talked about the woman in the convalescent home, that's all He wants. So many of our priests and religious don't even believe in the Real Presence anymore. What a heartache, huh? For God to become man was a gift that we would have never dreamed of, let alone that He reduces Himself even more and humbles Himself even more by coming to us as our food. How unbelievable! And yet we never even think of visiting Him. It seems like, in some parishes, they want to get Him as far away from His House as possible. If your children came in and said, "Okay, look, you've been good. Move. We'll build you a little shack next to the kitchen, and you stay there. The house is ours." I mean, you wouldn't even think of doing such a thing, you see? But, we're doing this to Jesus everywhere. We hide Him, we put Him in closets, we put Him outside. It's just like we don't even want Him to have His own temple.

If you want to give a gift to Jesus, I would suggest, you might even say, "Once a week, I'm going to make a visit to my church; I'm going to sit there and keep Him company." "I'm going to genuflect before I receive Jesus in the Eucharist." If you can't genuflect, bow. Why? Acknowledge His Presence. "I'm going to kneel for the Consecration." Why? Because that great miracle comes when Jesus, the Son of God, comes down into bread and wine. And they are transformed into the Body and Blood of Jesus. "I'm going to love His Mother this year. I'm going to say a Rosary once a day" or even once a week.

We owe the Lord our lives, our gifts, our talent, our jobs. Everything we do, we owe to Jesus. Everything comes from Jesus, from the Father through Jesus. And we owe Our Lady so much for saying yes, for being at the Cross, for being a comfort to Him. We are the ones who crucified Him, and she comforted Him. She gave Him strength. And she gave Him herself. She suffered every pain He suffered. You can't go through your whole life and ignore that kind of love. You can't.

A nice thing to give would be a basket of food or a toy to a needy family. The Father gave Jesus to us. We give something to Jesus. And we say at least, "Thank You, Father, for giving us—for giving me—Your Son."

Please visit Jesus. And be sure you tell Him you're going to be good next year.

Gifts for Jesus

If you wonder what you can give Jesus for Christmas, He deserves the first gift. I would think Confession would be a wonderful gift. Communion would be a wonderful gift. To get up Christmas morning, not running down to see what you got, but just to say, "Happy birthday, Jesus." See, let Him be first in your mind Christmas morning. Wouldn't that be nice?

Go to Midnight Mass. And I don't understand people who go to Midnight Mass, then go to a party and get drunk. What's wrong with you? Does anybody understand that? I'll bet a nickel you went to Confession, to Communion, went home, and got drunk. Now, does that make any sense? After you're drunk, you don't know what day it is. What's the purpose? You don't know. You're out like a light. You could wake up New Year's Day, and you wouldn't know what happened for a week. You see, we just do dumb things, that's all.

You could say a Rosary. I bet some of you haven't said a Rosary since Vatican II. I bet you don't even have one. But see, that would be a nice thing for you to do.

You might want to call an enemy, a person you haven't spoken to for a long time, and say, "Hey, I'm sorry. I'm very sorry. Please forgive me." Wouldn't that be a gift for Jesus? Wouldn't that be a gift of gifts?

You might want to call your mother-in-law. Why not? Say, "Well, I'm here. I know you're not too happy about it, but here I am, and I love you. You may be a battle-ax, but I love you." I don't think she'd appreciate it. You better skip that last part. But she may just be waiting for you to say hello, see?

Why don't you call a friend or visit a friend who's in a nursing home or just call him up if you're too far away? Oh, there's a thousand things you can give to Jesus for His birthday.

And I would like to mention one more. Would you say hello to His Mother? Would you say, "Thank you, Mary, for saying, 'Be it done to me according to Thy word' and for bearing the Son of the Most High God. Thank you"?

You know, we do thank Jesus, and we should, but let's not forget to thank His Mother on Christmas Day. And thank Him for His love, His peace, joy, and forgiveness.

The Best Gift for Jesus

If you really know it's Christmas, His birthday, the best gift you can give Jesus for His birthday is to go to Confession. That's what He wants. He wants to come back into your heart and soul. He wants you to open the door of your heart and take Him in and say, "Welcome, Lord. I'm sorry You've been gone so long. I'm sorry I've been such a sinner. I'm sorry I've ignored You. I'm sorry I didn't know You were around. I'm sorry I didn't give You attention. I'm sorry I didn't give You any love. I'm sorry I'm not grateful, Lord. I'm so sorry."

And so I'm hoping this Christmas will be your best. I'm hoping that you make it His best, that you give Him the gift He wants, not the gift *you* want:

that between now and then, you'll go to Confession. And then won't it be Christmas, huh, when Jesus will come into the little stable of your heart and lie in that manger and feel at home again? It would be a lot better than celebrating a season.

We shouldn't be afraid. You cannot be ashamed of Jesus' birth. You know, I know a lot of people have different religions or no religion, and they resent it. And that's okay. We're supposed to live in a free country, and I think we have the privilege of celebrating our religion, our God's birthday.

That's what Christmas is all about: to know Whose birthday it is. And I want to congratulate all of you who have not forgotten Whose birthday it is and that that's what Christmas is all about. If all the Catholics and Christians in this country did the same, wouldn't it be a change? I don't think it's hard to convert a whole nation. If the people love Jesus, they'll convert. If we know Jesus and we love Jesus, there's nothing too hard for us—*nothing*. And we can accept pain.

One season, I was in the hospital for Christmas, and I gave it to the Lord. It was obviously what He wanted. And the sisters put the telephone in the chapel. I heard the whole Midnight Mass over the phone, and after Mass was over, they all said hi and Merry Christmas, and they sang for me, and I felt at home. But I was all by myself in this room. It was very quiet that night, and I had a little crib, and you know, it was one of the best Christmases I had. Why? Well, you know, I heard Midnight Mass, I was there with the sisters, and most important, I was alone with the Child Jesus, with God. It was His birthday, and we were together in a lonely place on His birthday. I had a realization of His birth greater than any other day of my life.

And I think all of you who are alone and really suffer because of it, maybe you're not alone, huh? I'm sure you're not. You could have the best Christmas of your life, like I did, because you're celebrating the real reason.

Every Christmas Eve, we have the table decorated. We have Jesus right there as a Child, and we sing "Happy Birthday to You," because that's what we're celebrating, see, the Father's gift.

How to Approach Christmas When a Loved One Is Suffering

There's no question that it's hard to celebrate Christmas when a loved one is suffering. But you see, you have something that maybe a lot of people don't have. Sometimes we match love for love. Sometimes we match joy for joy. And now you have the opportunity of matching pain for pain.

You see, when the Infant was born, it was so cold. And that Infant was born in a cave, which meant the front was entirely open, so the wind wouldn't just pass it. It would be so cold in that cave. The rock was cold. So Mary suffered. Joseph suffered by the fact that he could provide no better than it was. And

Jesus was born in the cold. How did they handle that Christmas? How did Mary handle it? Well, she took the pain and wrapped her Son in her arms, and she made Him warm. But she was still cold.

And that's what you have to do: match pain for pain. That's how you're going to celebrate Christmas: with anticipation because He's coming. The One Who heals is coming, the One Who saves is coming, the One Who loves you is coming. For that reason, you should be joyful, not with an exuberant joy perhaps, but knowing that you have something to give the Christ Child that perhaps not too many people have.

You're also cold because you're afraid. You're lonely, as He was lonely, because nobody wanted Him. And all the turkey and all the trees suddenly have become very barren and unimportant. Well, now, you have an opportunity of living the same spirit that Mary and Joseph and Jesus had—a spirit of sacrifice, a spirit of love, a spirit of compassion. And you can still say from the bottom of your heart, "Infant Jesus, give us a spirit of love and sacrifice, and heal my loved one." The Infant is very powerful. My mother had great devotion to the Infant Jesus, especially the Infant of Prague. So pray to Him and ask Him to heal.

Losing a Loved One Before Christmas

If you lose a loved one before Christmas, I think you're going to miss them. There's no way you can't. I think the first Christmas without that person is always the hardest one. We can be consoled, but we can't be filled yet, see? That's the straw that you want to give to Jesus for His crib. "He came into His own, and His own received Him not. But to as many as received Him, He gave the gift of life" (see John 1:11–12).

You're kind of in a position of Jesus when He came. You're missing someone very dear. When He came, He missed a lot of people who were also very dear. And there was no one but a few shepherds and a couple of Wise Men later on. So you have something very precious to give to Jesus: a cross for a cross, a pain for a pain, love for love. I would give Him that this Christmas. I don't think there's much you can do. You're going to miss them. You can be consoled by thinking that they are with the real Infant; that they see Him in a way that we don't see Him; that they have a joy that is beyond every joy; that they see a sight more beautiful than anything we could imagine. Eye has not seen, nor ear heard what your loved one will see this Christmas. You and I have to wait, but He's worth waiting for.

Losing Your Temper

Okay, you feel kind of guilty, I think, for maybe taking out your frustrations on other people or something, and that's a temptation for everybody. But this is where I think Christmas comes in. You see, when Jesus came and there was no one there but His Mother and His foster father and a few shepherds, He didn't take it out on them. He was the same wonderful, loving God Who came unto His own, even though they didn't receive Him, even though they were cold and indifferent and just not around and not caring.

And that's what happens when people are nasty to you, especially at work. You may be working hard, doing a good job. Your boss is out of sorts or somebody you work with is out of sorts, and they take it out on you. And then you get angry, and you take it out on somebody else, and it just keeps going and going and going.

If we're Christian, somewhere it has to stop. See, we have to let that pattern stop at us and not go any further. We have to give that to the Lord. That's your straw this Christmas. A sister said something to me today, I forget what it was, and I said to her, "Oh, go and put another straw in." I have a feeling she didn't appreciate that too much, but anyway, that was my answer. So, just tell Jesus now you're sorry and you're going to try and do better next time, and put a straw in your crib.

How Jesus Elevates Our Life

Really the only gift that you and I can give to Jesus is our sins and our will. That's all that's mine. Everything else I have comes from Him. My sins are my own, and my will is my own, through His grace. He gave me free will. I can say no, even to God. Isn't that awesome? I can say no, even to God. He won't force me. That's why repentance is such a wonderful, wonderful gift. And some of you need to be repentant. And maybe tonight you'd like to say, "I repent of this, or I want to."

Do you know this woman called once, and she said she asked us to pray she would be repentant over something that had hurt her so much. We need to pray for repentance sometimes; in today's world, you don't even know when you've committed a sin because everybody says, "Oh, nah, that's okay. As long as you love, that's all right." But it's not! It's not all right. There's some little voice down there in your conscience that tells you, "No, no! That's not the right thing to do." But you squash it like you put out a light on a candle. So, don't do that. If the Lord is calling you between now and Christmas to repentance, that's what you want to do.

Then you say, "Well, Lord, I don't know what to be repentant of." Whoa, you're in bad shape! But you're in good shape if you know you're in bad shape. That came out pretty good, didn't it?

In today's world, where there is so much abortion, we've lost the concept of life. In today's world, where euthanasia is being pushed so hard, we lose the concept of life. Where there is so much tragedy, where there are such civil wars and such atrocities, we lose the reality and the value of life. And as we look at the Bible, you know, we've got to see the value of life, because the Word became flesh. If the Eternal Word became flesh, then you get a concept of the value of life. See, if you miss that, that's why there are so many abortions; you lost the concept of the value of life. But if you did, then remember that the Son of God came down to be human, and that elevates our life. He came down to work. That elevates our work. Even if you're just sweeping a floor, it's somehow holy. Every kind of work has been made holy by Jesus.

Pain. Pain is something that's awful and horrible, and some would kill people if they were in pain, like they would a dog. But Our Lord elevated suffering and pain because He went through it. People want to kill themselves because they may have a painful death. But Our Lord elevated a painful death by going through it. And then, to give us courage, He rose from the dead to make us realize it's worth it all! So we have to have that reality of the beauty and the preciousness of life in any form, whether it's a suffering child, or a suffering adult, or a suffering old person. We have to understand that beauty of our work, and how valuable it is and what a gift it is to work; so many of you without work realize what a gift it is to work.

So, when Jesus came, He took everything that's mundane and everything that's human and, to many, gross—He took it all, and He elevated it, and He made it holy. He made it beautiful. He made it good. So you have to handle life like it was something very precious and fragile, like earthenware jars, St. Paul says (see 2 Cor. 4:7).

Thanking God for the Incarnation

As creatures of God, as servants of the Lord, as His brothers and sisters, we must bring forth in us, according to season, Our Lord's entire life. Why? Because He came. He needs to be thanked. He needs to be loved.

The Father needs to be thanked in my heart. He needs to hear me say that I am so happy He's coming, that He's here. And all of time is present to God. Maybe billions and billions of people in the past said "Thank You" to Him. But *I* need to say it. I am the one He created. I am the one who lives alone with God. And God treats me as if no one else existed. And remember that one attribute of the Lord: Everything is now. There's no past and no future. Everything is now.

And so, as a religious, as one who has been called by God to be a spouse of Jesus, I need to recall Our Lord's life. And that's what the Church does: She recalls His birth, recalls His baptism, recalls His circumcision, recalls His Passion, recalls His life, recalls His mission. I must recall that so that I can live that life. I must live the life of Jesus.

I need to be reborn. There's something in me not like the Father, not like Jesus, not like the Spirit. I must be reborn. But I must look at that birth of Jesus, that wondrous, awesome gift from God the Father, I must look at it and give Him praise and honor and glory, because He did it. And He did it for me. I can never take any part of the life of Jesus and push it aside as if it weren't important. And that happens a lot. That's why I wear a cross. I can't forget what He did for me. It's present to the Father. That's what every Mass is—not another sacrifice; it's the *same* sacrifice. It is visible, always present to the Father. I am present there. And so it is with the birth of Christ.

See, with the birth of Jesus, I need to be present; I need to thank the Father for this wondrous gift.

And that's why we go through Lent, and that's why we cry on Good Friday, because He died for my sins. I need to express my sorrow, my love, my joy when He rises so that every part of Jesus' life is a part of me. And although it's good to look for the Second Coming—every time I hear the news, I look for Him to come, and I wish He'd come now—you can never push aside His entire life. It's not gone. It's always present to the Father. And it affects me, in my time, in this age, where I am—from His birth, to His life, as a Minister of God the Father, of constantly proclaiming the Father, to His death and Resurrection, and the coming of the Holy Spirit. I must live that life in my daily life. Otherwise, I'll miss the boat.

"Season's Greetings"

You see more and more signs that say "Season's Greetings." Well, what does that mean? Are we celebrating winter? I mean, that's the season, is it not? This is the winter season. When you say, "Season's greetings," what do you say—"Happy winter to you"? Who wants to say "Happy winter"? Winter's never happy. It's freezing! It's the world saying, "So much for you. Season's greetings!"

Up north, they have snow, and they're sliding this way and that way. And you say, "Oh, that's fun!" Well, I never thought it was fun. I was blue. My legs were blue when I'd walk to school, three miles, and I didn't think it was fun at all. So, I would never say "Season's greetings." And now they have cards with a big snowman. Are you celebrating snowman season? Because it says, "Season's Greetings." Then they have sleighs. Maybe we're celebrating sleigh time. Oh, then they always have a winter scene, you know, where people are in the sleigh and they're going their way, but that says "Season's Greetings" also.

Now I know the Eastern Rites, and the letter *X* means "Christ"; that's fine. But now we don't even want to write "Christmas" out. We put "Xmas." Well, I know that says "Christmas," but very few people who say "Merry Christmas" mean "Have a happy *Christ*mas." The Incarnation is among us, see. And you see lights on streets. That's fine, but if a city puts a crib up, then they get sued, you see, because it's something about Church and state. You know that monkey business. So we're not really allowed to put something up that says, "I'm celebrating the birthday of the Messiah."

And I wonder, and I'm sure you wonder, why are we ashamed or afraid to say "Christmas"? Whose birthday is it—the winter's? No. Santa Claus's? No. That's St. Nicholas, and his feast has already come.

Christmas is the Father's gift to us. And we never give Jesus a gift. Do you give Jesus a gift for Christmas? Whose birthday is it? I don't know if we know any-more Whose birthday it is. See, what we're supposed to celebrate is the birth of Jesus, the Son of God.

On Christmas Eve here, we always sing "Happy Birthday" to Jesus and all during Advent, we try to do something for Him, make a gift of myself to Jesus, see. We've lost the whole reality of the birthday of Jesus, and you have everything except that. See, why do you buy a gift for somebody at Christmas? Why don't you do it on February 10? It's just as good a day as anything else. Why don't we do it another day? No, we pick the birthday of Jesus to give each other gifts. Well, I suppose it's a good thing. You're imitating the Father. But are we imitating the Father, or is it just a happy season? It's a season for giving gifts.

And have you noticed that they start around the middle of November with Christmas trees? When I was a young kid, we could never put a Christmas tree up until, oh, about a week before Christmas be-cause we knew what we were celebrating. And then, on December 26, walk downtown, and you'll find all those Christmas trees out in the street. They're finished now. They're going to have a big white sale. What's a white sale? Sheets. Well, why do you want sheets? Sheets, pillow cases, towels—so we're all mixed up. See, the season is to put your tree up the night before Christmas, and you keep it up until the sixth of January because that's the season for His birth, for the Magi coming.

See, we're not liturgical at all. We're commercial. I'll make a bet that beautiful tree that you spent a week on and probably spent a couple hundred dollars with decorations will come down the twenty-sixth of December because your season's over. Oh, that shouldn't be. It took hundreds and hundreds of years for Him to come. We have to celebrate it at least a couple of weeks.

Being Alone on Christmas

You know, I bet the people who are alone on Christmas are the only ones celebrating Christmas. Think about it. Women in lonely apartments. And maybe you are lonely, and maybe you're crying because there's nobody around and everybody's celebrating. But maybe you're the only one celebrating. Maybe you're the one who really knows Whose birthday it is.

When my mother was alone after I entered the monastery, for Christmas she was alone, but she had two plates on her table, one for her and one for Jesus. You say, "Oh, come on now; He wasn't there." Yeah, He was, in spirit. He appreciated that she knew it was His birthday, and she celebrated His birthday. And she'd go across the street to St. Peter's and spend the entire afternoon in Adoration.

Well, in the eyes of the world, she was a lonely woman, all by herself on this great feast of Christmas, but I wonder if she wasn't one of the few who understood Whose birthday it was and spent the afternoon with Him. You see, we have lost the reality of why He came, and so we don't celebrate why He came. So I would like to just go over a little bit of St. Luke's Gospel, because I would like to get into your hearts before the great day comes the beauty of Christmas.

Appreciating the Coming of Our Savior

You and I were saved when He came. The salvation of the world, the redemption of the world began when Mary said, "Be it done to me according to Thy will," and there He was through the power of the Holy Spirit (see Luke 1:38). That's what you're celebrating. The prophets wrote about it, Isaiah especially, and men and women for centuries thought about it, prayed about it, prayed it would come soon. And hundreds of years passed, and suddenly there He was. But where was He? In a stable. You see, even then we didn't understand. There was nobody there but a few shepherds.

And you know, shepherds in those days were not the cleanest people in the world. Well, we wouldn't say they smelled bad, but I bet they did. I bet if they were out in a field night after night, day after day, they were in the mud, they were in the rain. They didn't go home and take a little shower. I mean, they were dirty. And not only were they smelly, you hate to say, these beautiful shepherds you got in your Nativity scene were smelly, but what happens to you if you don't take a bath every day? I mean, it's pretty bad. They didn't have deodorant. But these men came as they were. They didn't say, "Well, I better dress up," you know. And you can't have five, ten animals in a cave and have it smell good.

See, we don't understand what Jesus did for us, because He was not welcomed in this world He came to save. He wasn't welcomed. We have no room in the inn. And that's what we're saying today, "Season's greetings." You don't have room in your inn for Him. We don't have room. We're busy about many, many things.

Well, I'm not against gifts. Someone sent me three boxes of dates. I don't know where they got them. I mean, I never saw a date that big. If you eat one of those, you have a meal. Well, I'm grateful for them. I get them every Christmas.

But you see, it's not my birthday. It's *His* birthday. And I know everybody's sending me gifts, and we gobble it up. I got big salami tonight–and it's Italian–and I was so excited. And somebody sent us pastrami too. I said to Sister, "Cut them thin; it will last longer." And I appreciate all these gifts, and I know it's given in the right intention, but a lot of people don't have the right intention.

Well, let's just start here a little bit. We all know that the angel came to Mary and said, "The power of the Most High will cover you with His shadow," and we can't even imagine what that meant (Luke 1:35). The Spirit of the Lord, the third Person of the Blessed Trinity, came and overshadowed Mary, and there He was, the One awaited for centuries, and they all missed Him. He was in their midst, and they knew it not. And I've got to ask you, and I have to ask myself the same question. He is in our midst: Do we know it, or do we know it not? You know, it would be a shame if we didn't. And I'm sure, when we read this: "He came unto His own, and His own received Him not" (John 1:11, Douay-Rheims), isn't it true today when you forget Whose birthday it is, when you forget why He came?

Today you don't think you have any sin. There's no sin in the world today. Big sinners are excused. If I were a man, I'd be insulted today. I'm a woman, and I'm insulted today because women are not considered women. They're considered vehicles of pleasure and trash. You cannot go, you cannot watch, you can't go through the channels, even to get the news, without seeing how women dress and how they're considered by the producers who produce trash. They're half dressed—actually, if they were half dressed, I'd be happy. They'd be well dressed if they were half dressed, and you consider that something wonderful. You don't even know when you're being insulted. That's what's so bad.

And men, well, if someone can commit the most terrible sins and lust and people say, "He's only a man," that means the rest of you are in the same boat. That's not a compliment. It's not a compliment to be considered trash. See, but we treat Jesus the same way. You can't help treating each other the same way. No, because we don't know Who came to us and why. The Father felt so much pity for us that He sent His Son to redeem us under such trying circumstances—in a cave He's born, wrapped with swaddling clothes, cold, then having to run away from who? A king who was insane, filled with disease.

You know why Herod died? Well, he decided he was a god. A lot of people decide they're gods today. And he had made for him a gold gown. When he went out and talked to the people, the gold shone in the sun, so bright. And they said, "Ah, behold a god!" And he sat down, and suddenly his gown began to move on him. You know what was moving under that gown? Maggots. The man was dying in front of their faces, in front of their eyes, and before he died, the maggots were already eating him up. So much for that king.

You see, he didn't know that a Child was born, a Child was given to us to save us. There he died, a miserable wretch who never accepted his God, who was so jealous and ambitious that he had all the children who were up to two years old slaughtered. And then he made a law that the moment he died, all the sons of all the wealthy and all the kings would be killed. Why? So somebody would cry the day he died. Now you say, "That is terrible!" Oh, come on, what are we doing today? On Christmas Day, there will be slaughtered some young babies in their mothers' wombs, I'll make a bet, and we don't care because we're celebrating a season. Are we any better than the ones who were there for the First Coming? And will we be any better when He comes a second time?

You say, "Are you going to bring that up?" Yeah, I'm going to bring it up. You don't need to listen to me, but you're going to because you're curious. You want to know what I'm going to say next. And what I'm going to say is this: I don't think we're much better than we were the first time because we're too interested in the season.

Well, let's see what He's interested in. We all know that Our Dear Lady went to visit Elizabeth, and then it says, "There was a time when Caesar Augustus issued a decree for a census." You know, when David ordered a decree, he was punished by the Lord. "And everyone went to his own town to be registered" (Luke 2:1, 3). I'd like to see Joseph when he went up to the captains or soldiers, and the soldier would look up.

He says, "Name, please."

"Joseph."

"What tribe?"

"David."

"Is that your wife?"

"Yes."

"Go on."

Have you any idea what that soldier missed? He was talking to the foster father of the Son of God. He was saying, just like any other, "Is that your wife?" "Yes." "Go on." He talked to Our Lady. Who wouldn't give their arm and front teeth to talk to Our Lady? He missed the chance of a lifetime. And within her was Jesus, Son of God, but all he was interested in is the census.

Making Time for Jesus

And all we're interested in is the season. Is there any difference? Well, I'm sure Joseph thought He had enough relatives there, somebody would take him in, but they're all too busy. Are we? Christmas is creeping up on us. We're all so busy. Do we know what's going to happen? Are we like that soldier: "Name? Address? Tribe? Go on"? Are we like that? Well, it looks like it, because he goes on, and it says, "While they were there, the time came for her to have her Child. And she gave birth to a son, her firstborn. She wrapped Him in swaddling clothes and laid him" (Luke 2:6–7)—where? In a nice, comfortable bed with a wool blanket in a warm house? No. In a drafty, windy cave with prickly straw. And the awesome thing about it is that Our Lady was content, and so was Joseph. Why? Because they had Jesus. The birth of the Son of God had to be awesome.

We don't always realize what happened. We believe that since Our Lady remained a virgin before and after that, the Son of God came through her little tummy like He did at the Resurrection. He already was risen when the angels rolled that stone back. He came through the stone, like He went through the door when the apostles were talking about Him, and suddenly, with the door locked, He was standing there. And some of the great mystics have told us that at the scene of the birth of Christ, Michael and Gabriel were there to hand Him to His Mother, and there in her arms suddenly was the Son of God.

Awesome! The first birthday of the Lord Messiah, the first birthday, and it was cold, and nobody was there but Joseph and Mary.

And tonight in most places in the world, it's cold, and there's nobody there but Jesus and Mary. We haven't changed very much. We're too interested in the world, in the things of the world, and we don't know that He has come among us.

And then it says, "[The shepherds] were terrified, but the angel said, 'Do not be afraid. Listen, I bring you news of great joy, a joy to be shared by the whole people' " (Luke 2:9–10). Do you hear what it says? The angel appeared to a few shepherds. They're the only ones he could find who weren't too busy, just sitting around talking. Maybe they were talking about the Messiah. Maybe they're sitting there wondering in the middle of the night, "Will He ever come? Are things always going to be like this?" And then suddenly there was a great light, and they didn't know what was happening, and they were petrified. Wouldn't you be? I hope you'd be. I would be. If you looked up into the sky and the whole sky was lit up at midnight, and you saw angels up there, and they were singing their hearts out?

I bet there had to be one deaf shepherd, and he's saying, "What's he saying?" They say, "Oh, shut up. We don't know ourselves." I write my own Scripture. I made it up.

"He said, 'It's going to be great joy.' "

"Over what?"

"Well, listen. Shut up, and I'll tell you what."

"He said, 'The Messiah's here.' "

"No."

"Yeah."

"Well, where is He?"

"In some cave."

"A cave? The Messiah in a cave?"

"Yeah, He's like us—poor, unknown, unheralded, unaccepted by His own."

But the angel said, "The whole people should know."

Do you know? You're part of the whole people. Do you know Whose birthday it is? It says here, "I bring news of great joy, a joy shared by all the people.

Today, in the town of David, a saviour has been born to you. He is Christ the Lord. And here is a sign." (Luke 2:11–12).

You know, we're always asking for signs, a sign for this and a sign for that. In fact, you can't travel unless you have a sign. You wouldn't know it was east, west, north, or south. "You will find a baby wrapped in swaddling clothes." So far, that's no different from any other baby—lying, though, in a manger (Luke 2:12). That's different. No baby lies in a manger.

Today, they have garbage cans. That what you have for babies today, garbage cans—or you sell them, you sell them for money. You get money for abortion, then you get money from another scientist because he wants to operate on their brains. He wants to take something out of their bodies. No, we have garbage cans today. We don't have cribs and mangers. Yeah, we know how to do it. We make Herod look good. Oh, no.

"And suddenly with the angel there was a great throng of the heavenly host, praising God. 'Glory to God in the highest heaven and peace to men who enjoy His favor' " (Luke 2:13–14).

Well, those shepherds found Jesus. See, they hurried away and found Him in the manger. Are you looking for Jesus? Are you looking for the Anointed One? Are you looking for the one the prophets spoke about? Are you looking for the Savior, or don't you need one? You don't need one, huh? I can tell you, buddy, you need one bad, but He's come. He's come in our midst. He's in the Eucharist. You can go to any Catholic Church, and He's there. I hope He's there. I hope and pray you will go to your church on Christmas Day and say, "Happy birthday, Lord. I'm so glad You came. I'm glad You're here. I'm grateful that You saved me."

Christmas

The Gifts of the Magi

Now, tradition has it that Our Dear Lady and St. Joseph gave away to the poor the gifts of the Magi: the gold, the myrrh, and the frankincense. They were valuable. And they gave them away. If you remember, they had to run to Egypt because Herod was after the Child and wanted to kill Him.

Today, we have a similar thing, and we call it abortion. It's a different kind of king, a different kind of Herod that runs, searching for little children, to do away with them. Herod did away with them out of ambition. He was afraid that this Person would take his place. But the same thing is happening today, everywhere, in a different way, but the same idea. "This child is going to spoil something in my life."

"This child is going to take away my comfort." "This child is going to be an expense." "This child is going to take away my career." And as a result, we do the same thing today. We get rid of them—as Herod got rid of all those children up to two years old. We don't even allow them to be born, because they're in the way. And that's the same thing that's happened now, and it happened then.

And so Our Lady and St. Joseph would never have kept all that the Magi gave them. They wouldn't have had a place for it. And they wouldn't have been using it for the next twenty years. They gave it as they would have given everything else they had. They knew that this Child, born in a stable, wanted to be poor.

The Mighty God Comes as a Little Child

 want to read you two things now—first, from the Prologue of the Gospel of St. John; then I'm going to read to you from Isaiah 9:5–6.

St. John says, "In the beginning was the Word" (1:1). Wow! In the very beginning—well, there was no beginning, really, with God, but we don't know how to express "no beginning," so we say it's the beginning—there was the Word, "and the Word was with God, and the Word was God" (1:1). How do you like that? The knowledge the Father has of Himself is the Word.

Well, if you look in Isaiah 9:5–6, we find something else. He says, "For there is a child born for us."

For us. So Jesus is born *for us*. Can you imagine that? He came just for me. The Little Flower—we call her St. Thérèse of the Child Jesus—she used to look out in the woods, and she'd say, "That tree is just for me, and that rock is just for me. He knew that someday I would be standing beneath that tree and be looking at it and saying, 'How great Thou art!' " You see, we don't know how close God is to us; neither do we know how much He loves us. Do you know that? No, we don't know that because the only thing we know is human love, and it gets a little shaky sometimes, see? So we judge God's love by human love, and that's a mistake. He's always there.

Well, now Isaiah says, "For there is a child born for us, a son given to us." He's given—by the Father. The Son, the Eternal Word, came down, was made flesh in the womb of that wondrous woman we call Mary, "and dominion is laid on His shoulders. And this is the name they give Him." You know, when you love somebody, you have all kinds of sweet names. Is that what you do? When you were courting, did you have cute names? Well, here's the name Jesus is talking about. He's "Wonder-Counsellor." Oh, wow! "Mighty-God, Eternal-Father, Prince-of-Peace"!

You know, so many people need a counselor today, and they need a consoler. Don't you think people need a consoler? Oh, everybody is heartbroken about just about everything. Something's happening in the Church; then there are all of these other things going on in the world and revolutions. And there is no use in getting depressed. It's all in the hand of God, right there! You say, "Well if it's all right there, how come it's so bad?" We made it bad. But He's got it all together. That's why He's Mighty God! We can trust and ask Mighty God.

You know, sometimes we forget that He's Mighty God. Sometimes we forget that He's God in the flesh, and we can't ever forget that! Mary didn't forget that! And you know, when Philip said, "Show us the Father, Lord," Jesus said, "He who sees me sees the Father" (see John 14:8–9). He's the Alpha and the Omega, the beginning and the end (Rev. 21:6). He's everything! And He's all in a little package about *that* big. You can't, I can't, imagine that. I sometimes sit in the chapel, and I try to meditate on this great God who created the whole universe out of a word! He said, "Let there be light," and *boom!* There was light (Gen. 1:3)!

Now, some of you scientists out there who think you're so smart, I think you're trying to figure it out, see? You're going to find, when you meet Him face-to-face, it was just that easy. See, scientists sometimes have to see if things are in order, and then they've got to put them all together. First, they have a big bang thing, a theory, and now they threw that out the window—threw it out in the universe somewhere. And they have all kinds of other theories, but God doesn't have to work in parts and sections and categories. He just says, "Let there be," and there is! He's the Eternal Father, Mighty God, and He never changes. And the most wonderful thing, I think, is His love never changes.

How to Appreciate the Lord Jesus Christ's Coming as a Child

We have to realize, number one, what it must have meant for Jesus Christ to come as a Child. And we can't realize because, you see, we don't have a reality of the Godhead, and we don't know what it means to be God. We don't realize what it means to be so powerful that we could say to darkness, "Be light," and it changes! Or to be so powerful that we could create a star or a universe or a galaxy or quasar. We don't understand what that means. We don't understand what it means to make a mountain or a river or an ocean or fish or animals. And because we don't have that concept, it's difficult for us to say that Someone who could do all of that became a Child. Wow!

I have a little heart pill that I take twice a day. If I were to tell you that I'm going to take all the oceans and all the rivers and all the lakes and all the wells, and I'm going to take every drop of water on the earth and in the skies—I'm going to take all of that and I'm going to put it in this pill, what would you think? You'd say, "Uh huh!" But it's nothing, absolutely nothing, compared with what God did! Absolutely nothing that this gigantic God—and there's usually not a word for Him because how can you describe God? You can't! He came *that* small. Listen! See, I can hardly hold this pill, it's so small. It's nothing. We can begin a little bit to realize what He did when He became man. And just on Christmas morning, wherever you are, think of that.

Silence and Trust

God does great things, great things in unknowns and in silence. But we are a generation of noise. We are not happy. You can't even get in an elevator without songs and music and noise. People put radios on, turn TVs on, and they are not looking at anything and are not listening. It seems that we have forgotten the silence. And that's where God can work best—in silence. And that's why you suddenly feel that need to go from all the noise we have every day—every day and every moment of the day—to the silent presence.

See, God's presence is silent. And I know He made quite a noisy Pentecost—you know, the wind and the house shaking—but that was only to wake us up because we need something like that. We used to have silence in church, but even now, in church, right after Mass, we have to start talking. There is no way now, no way in our life, with our neighbor and family, to arrive at that silence.

No matter who you are or where you are or what you believe, God's presence comes forth in a powerful way in silence—now, in your homes, in this little place right now, if you just let your ears be aware. See, our ears are not aware of silence. Silence can be very loud. But a silence that comes from prayer is very soft, very quiet. If you remember, Elijah went up the mountain, and he didn't hear God in the thunderstorm or the earthquake, and suddenly, he said that there was a tiny breeze, and there was God, you see (1 Kings 19:11–13).

I think we are afraid of that. It seems like we are very afraid of silence. And when we have noise, we can forget our sinfulness. We can sin more with ease because it's so noisy and loud, we don't have time to think. It's a hidden agenda of the enemy to make it as noisy as possible. People sin much easier then. They see others sin, and that gives them more courage to go on sinning, but it's the wrong kind of courage, you see. And as soon as there is any kind of silence, they get squirmy. They are very uneasy.

It's not only silence of mind, though. See, I think we are always thinking of the mind. It's a silence of the heart combined with the silence of the mind—because God dwells in your heart, your soul.

There is a silence of the mind that means your memory is quiet, perhaps. Your intellect is not wondering and wishing and analyzing, and your will is pretty placid. You haven't made up your mind to do anything, or you have, and you quieted down. The silence of the heart, though, is when you know this is His birthday, and you know you must give Him a gift, and the gift is your love. God has manifested to you, in this little Baby, His power, His creative power, and His love, you see. And there is no fear in Christmas.

You know, you could be pretty well petrified seeing Our Lord hanging on the Cross, but at Christmas, He takes away all the fear of the heart, and you begin to wonder. There's where the wonder in your heart about God becoming man comes from. Why would He do that? And it's such a high mystery, you cannot think of it. You cannot put it in your mind because it's a mystery of God. So unless you connect with the Child Jesus, heart to heart, you cannot understand the mystery.

Now, when the heart begins to contemplate, we can reason, we can meditate, and then we can contemplate. And the contemplation comes from the heart, not the mind. And what happens then is that you can gaze at this Little Child and say, "Ah, wow!" And you can stay there for a long time, you see. But we are so accustomed to analyzing and dissecting everything and making as much noise as possible that that contemplation of the heart is totally lost.

I've seen some saints in my life when I've gone to different places, and they all have that charism. You know that even if you are talking to them, their heart is somewhere else. And you've got their whole attention. It's not that they are ignoring you; they're not in some kind of ecstasy and ignoring you. But because their heart is with Jesus, because their heart is with that Presence, they can give you their total attention, you see. Some people—you know they are not listening. You know. And some people—Christmas goes right past them as fast as a train does. They know it's Christmas. They know it's His birthday, but they've lost it in their hearts.

Why don't we turn to the Magi—they are the ones who brought gifts—and then keep Christmas with that meditative, quiet time when the whole world must have been quiet. I could imagine everything in the world—even if it was midnight—I can imagine the wind stopping, and the leaves didn't move, and I bet the whole city felt something, but they didn't know what it was. That awesome time that people waited centuries for was suddenly there, and it was so quiet. I think that's why Our Dear Lord allowed His Son to be born in a cave. What more quiet place than a cave?

I think the reason the shepherds were surprised was not that the Messiah came but *how* He came. And these were men of silence. But they were also sinners. They knew they needed a Savior. But it's strange that Our Dear Lord called those who were basically unknown, uncared for, unloved, but, most of all, silent. They had to meditate a lot on God's creation. They were not scandalized by the cave. Isn't that odd? They were not at all scandalized. That's where they lived. And they understood.

But you see, we don't have any silent time with God. And I'm not talking about transcendental meditation and all that make-believe stuff. I'm talking about giving God some time in our life and beginning to see Him in everything. If I don't see Him in this little stroke, which is minor, then where am I going to go? There is no place to go except discouragement, anger, fear. See, we are so much in the world, we have become *of* the world. Our Lord said, talking about the apostles, "Father, I leave them in the world, but they cannot be of the world," and that's the whole point (see John 17:13, 16). Everybody is of the world besides being in the world. Now, the Christian, especially the Catholic who has the Eucharist and Confession, is in the world, but they have got to have time for God. They have to see Him with what they call the interior light. They have to see God in every single thing that happens around them and within them, and then there is no difference between joy and sorrow. That doesn't mean you are hee-hawing all day, but there is a peace and serenity that we have now in the midst of sorrow.

What aggravated the Sadducees and the Pharisees and some other people was the fact that Our Lord was so serene, even when He was before Pilate. That's what aggravated Pilate, and it made him wonder, "Who is this Man?" See, when Pilate got kind of arrogant, he said, "Don't You know that I can release You or crucify You?" And then Our Lord said, "No. You have no power over me except the Father gives to you" (see John 19:10–11). Why don't we think of that in the midst of our tragedies? Whether the tragedies of war, the tragedies in our own families, our own personal tragedies—why don't we think of that? This has to come from God!

One thing we've lost in the world is trust. We don't have that trust in God we should have. We are accustomed to having the world do so many things, new things, great things, sending men to the moon. And so it's almost as if the world has taken the place of God because it does great things. But people have lost the reality that, even in those things, God had to give them strength, courage, and life.

And what we are doing is putting our hearts and souls and our confidence in things that are before us or within us, and that doesn't last long. It disappears. That's why we can't accept suffering. Suffering is not a part of our human concept of joy and happiness, you see. That's why they divorce joy from sickness. They divorce joy from handicaps. They divorce joy from these tragic surprises. And I think that's one of the reasons we don't trust God. Our trust is in ourselves or things, and it passes.

Materialism

You know, the day after Christmas, everything comes down. We used to have what we called an octave. But now, the gifts are in; the gifts are out. Big sales—you've got to be there first for the white sale or the blue sale or the green sale.

See, we are materialistic. How can you know for sure—as we do—that Christ is born, the Son of God is here, and then throw everything out the day after? I don't understand that.

I think we need to pray during that day. I would advise families to do what my mother did when she was alone. Even if you have twenty people in your family, set a plate, a fork, a knife—everything everybody else has—for Our Lord and say, "That's Jesus.

That's for Him." You will be surprised what that little place by itself, just empty—you think it's empty, but I think He is there because you thought of Him—can do to calm everybody down.

My uncle said one day, "I'm not going over to your mother's for Christmas."

And I said, "Why not!"

He said, "I keep looking at that empty spot."

I said, "It's because you don't have any faith. That's what's wrong with you."

We need a reminder of what that peace is really about. But I would recommend that every family do something about that happy reminder, you see. Otherwise, we go into the material. But I think that empty space, if you keep looking at it, would calm the family down.

I thought of something that we can do: I remind the sisters, and as parents, you can look at your children two or three days before Christmas, and say, "He is coming! He is coming!" And during your meal or during the day on Christmas, why don't you get your kids to say, "He is here! The Lord God is here!"

I think that will give you confidence and trust because when He came, He meant to give us courage and strength and hope. And He said, "I leave you my joy, and no man can take it away" (see John 16:22). Isn't that wonderful? To the world, peace is the absence of chaos. To us who are Christian, that kind of joy is peace in the midst of chaos.

God bless you, and Merry Christmas.

Celebrating Christmas Without Family

Some people don't have family at all. And that's what makes Christmas and holidays so painful to a lot of people. There are single-parent families. There are single people who really don't have a family or a place to go. There is a certain amount of detachment that's good, inasmuch as if that is your state in life, if that's where you are at this moment, there still is no reason why you cannot be alive with that wonderful day we call the Birth of Christ.

So, detachment on that level is very good. But we still need our family. Whether they speak of the world or not, you still need to give them some Christmas cheer. Go at least to visit. You don't have to stay. But go at least to visit, and say, "Hey, this is the birthday of Christ." Maybe nobody ever told them it was His birthday.

I just learned recently that many of our Protestant brothers don't have any services on Christmas Day. Well, that would be sad for me, if we didn't have that opportunity to say, "Hi, Jesus. Happy birthday! I love You." And so, what I think you need to do is go for a visit and say, "Hey, it's Jesus's birthday. Why don't we say, 'Happy birthday, Jesus'?" And maybe they'll look at you and say, "Where'd you come from?" But you'll have planted a seed. And sometimes, that's all we need is a seed.

So don't just write them off. At the same time, know that, if you can, really spend the day. When my mother was alone, after I left for the monastery, she spent the whole day in church. She'd eat her dinner, then she'd go to church and stay there.

Well, I hope now you will have a better Christmas. And don't forget to sing Him "Happy Birthday." A cake may be in order too.

Depression and Loneliness at Christmas

We all have depressions. Around Christmastime, you might recall somebody who just died, and so they're not there to celebrate. There's all kinds of reasons why people feel sad at Christmas, but I think if we tried to just say, "Jesus, I'm so happy You were born in our midst. What would I do without You?," He would like to hear that.

I know you have great depression, but just think of Jesus for five minutes. Will you do that? And say, "Jesus, I can't feel You." But you don't need to feel God. It's a matter of will. It's a matter of wanting to know Jesus and to be happy He came. And ask Our Lady to teach you that wonderful lesson that we must be joy filled—not over ourselves, not over conditions. They change. You feel good one day; the next day, you feel terrible. The world is wonderful today, and the next day, it's terrible, see? We live in a changing world, but we must love the changeless One. You try it, huh?

You know, many people are asking for prayers for Christmas, and many people being laid off right after Christmas, many people are alone for Christmas, many are sick this Christmas. But I want you to look at Jesus, the Son of God, Who came at Christmas, and unite your pain, your loneliness, to His.

For centuries and centuries, people called and said, "When are You coming?" But when He came, there was no one there. That's loneliness, huh? When He came, nobody was interested, and that's what you suffer, isn't it? Oh, He wasn't sick, but there is a kind of loneliness that's a pain, a deep pain in the heart. Isn't that sickness of pain? Isn't that a part of loneliness?

All I'm asking is that you don't make a wrong choice. You say, "Life is not worth living." Yes, it is, for

His sake. Don't separate yourself from Him forever. Say, "Lord, You were alone in a cave, and I'm alone, and I love You, and I wish You a happy birthday." You'll be surprised what it will do for you.

See, you and He have a lot in common. And maybe that's why He was born in a stable. Maybe that's why His birth was a lonely one, a few shepherds, not at all the "Great King coming" or a parade or some great celebration. No, there was no one around. "He came unto His own, and His own received Him not." So, all of you who are in that condition, please think of Him.

Encouragement for the Lonely

I want to give a word of encouragement to all these people who are hurting because from the very moment of His existence, Jesus hurt. Oh, it wasn't physical. He was in the arms of Mary, and I can't think of anything more wonderful than that. He had gazed upon the beautiful face of St. Joseph and the innocence of those around Him. But you see, there's nothing worse than being hurt in love, really nothing. Some of you have been disappointed in love. Some of you have never loved. Some of you are afraid to love. And some of you feel alone this Christmas, and you don't want to do that. Jesus is with you. You're not alone when you're with Jesus. If you know you have Him right here, and you know that He loves you so much, that's the important thing! And I just ask Jesus to make everybody feel and understand that He loves you. *He loves you.* So, we just ask the Lord that you might give all the people who hurt the reality that He loves them.

We wish that the Infant Jesus just wraps you around and gives you peace and joy, the power of His Spirit, that you will realize what it meant for the Word to become flesh and dwell among us, that you will understand the depth and the height of His love for you, and that no matter how grateful or how ungrateful we are at this moment, He loves us. He loves me! He loves you! I wish you a very wondrous Christmas. God bless you!

Mother M. Angelica

(1923–2016)

Mother Mary Angelica of the Annunciation was born Rita Antoinette Rizzo on April 20, 1923, in Canton, Ohio. After a difficult childhood, a healing of her recurring stomach ailment led the young Rita on a process of discernment that ended in the Poor Clares of Perpetual Adoration in Cleveland.

Thirteen years later, in 1956, Sr. Angelica promised the Lord as she awaited spinal surgery that, if He would permit her to walk again, she would build Him a monastery in the South. In Irondale, Alabama, Mother Angelica's vision took form. Her distinctive approach to teaching the Faith led to parish talks, then pamphlets and books, then radio and television opportunities.

By 1980 the Sisters had converted a garage at the monastery into a rudimentary television studio. EWTN was born. Mother Angelica has been a constant presence on television in the United States and around the world for more than thirty-five years. Innumerable conversions to the Catholic Faith have been attributed to her unique gift for presenting the gospel: joyful but resolute, calming but bracing.

Mother Angelica spent the last years of her life cloistered in the second monastery she founded: Our Lady of the Angels in Hanceville, Alabama, where she and her nuns dedicated themselves to prayer and adoration of Our Lord in the Most Blessed Sacrament.